Also by Aura Levitas

Sisu

TIME
STEP

AURA LEVITAS

ARTWORK BY
AURA LEVITAS

THE VELLAMO PRESS
New York

ISBN: 1508604975
ISBN: 9781508604976

Printed in the United States of America

First Edition

For Willard
Whose presence is still felt
and whose support is always with me.

Contents

GROWTH

I am a different person now
From what I used to be.
It seems that I was dumber
And smart crept up on me.
You get to know a lot more words
And feel their meanings, too,
Like anger, hate and jealousy.
Depressed and feeling blue.
Of course, there are the other words;
The good ones, one might say.
Romance, success and honesty,
But most important, play.
I guess if we live long enough
We'll get smarter every day.
So let's use our smarts
And just 'play' dumb.
So be it, as it may.

DADDY AND COLE

Cigarette butts lay squashed
In an ashtray.
Sheet music was on the music rack.
It was Sunday afternoon
My Father's retreat from the pressures
Of his work week.
Another new Cole Porter song
Waited for him to play.
I sensed the music made him feel
Human and almost sophisticated.
Free of any antagonism for authority,
Unaware of the unhappiness
Felt by those closest to him.
Forgetful of the anger inside
For his mistaken life choices.
As he played, he recited the song.
He lit a cigarette.
The song had ended.
Yet it would be played over
And yet again.
I was grateful for Sundays and
Cole.
One song remains in my memory.
THANK YOU SO MUCH
MISSUS LOWSBOROUGH-GOODBY
Thank you Cole; thank you so much.

AN ONEIRIC VISITATION

An ethereal conversation
At the foot of my bed
Awakened me.
Whoever ceased their chatter
Sensing my presence.
Angels or aliens?
I cared not, as I so wanted
To become a
Believing companion.
As I reached for the light,
I heard a loud sneeze.
Fearing my dusty room
Had prompted the sneeze,
Made me moan.
So why had I been chosen
As the site for their tête-à-tête?
What was the reason for
Their immediate departure?
All at once I realized the reason.
It was my lack of good manners.
I had failed to say
GESUNDHEIT.

MISSED AND DISMISSED

MISSED

Middy blouses, Flame-Glo Lipstick
Chock full o nuts,
Saddle shoes, The Automat,
Dumbwaiters, Bingo, Double Features,
Mickey Mouse Watches,
Five and Dime Stores, Drive-ins.

What causes the good to disappear?
Replaced by barren settings
Of steel and glass
Robotic voices
And plastic fandangles.
Was it masked deciders
Who led the loss of good times?
Banishing them into thin air?
Leaving only recollections for us
For us to compare with
The furbelows and misery of today.

I remember the first day
I was permitted to wear lipstick.
I chose Flame-Glo Burnt Almond
And pouted my lips
So that everyone could see.

DISMISSED

Pigtails, Castor oil, Slam jackets, Girdles
Rubber Bathing Shoes, Popeye, Snoods.
Flashers, Inkwells, Galoshes. Babushkas
Silver Fox Jackets, Spam, Garter Belts,
Painted Turtles, Banana Cream Pie
Candy Cigarettes, Snoods, Howdy Doody

The elimination from our memory trove
Of uncomfortable apparel
And indignities to our
Taste and style
Is permissible.

LOVE IN ITS FINALITY

The boulder on which she sat
Was at the edge of a flowing stream.
Her toes dangled in the frigid water.
Love is like the water, she thought.
The white pebbles sparkled
With come hither looks
Wanting to be chosen
To be skimmed across the stream.
It seems that love surrounds me here.
Her thoughts remained on love.
The stream gurgled and gushed,
Rising to a roar as it approached
Its destiny, a waterfall.
Only to flail out wildly
Before descending into a
Pool of serenity and calmness.
Still splashing her toes,
Feeling love coming from below her
She sprinkled water on her face.
I am showered with kisses
She said aloud, smiling.
Gracefully sliding from
The boulder into the stream
Her eyes remained open
in the transparent water.
She lay amongst the pebbles.
Her last words, they could not hear.
I have missed being loved.
And neither can the pebbles cry.

NO MISTAKE ABOUT IT

There's no mistake about it.
Mistakes are here to stay.
They are defined as blunders.
But so many every day?

You wear a watch to shower.
It's not waterproof, of course.
You tip a cabbie, not enough
And live with the remorse.

You have a lunch date Tuesday,
And go Monday; wrong again.
There is a rather bright side, though,
You never missed a plane, but when?

We live our lives with stupid blunders
And daily try to not make more.
But who on earth would be so mean,
By keeping up a score?

PLAGUED

I've been
Held up, held down
Talked to, talked about
Cheated on, stood up
Lied to, lied about
Passed over, passed by
Overworked, underpaid
Spent a lot, lent a lot
Riled up, off guard.
I pay
Income tax, sales tax,
State tax, city tax
Water tax, sewer tax,
I avoid
Con men, petty thieves
Beggars, scams, liars
Even
Charities and lotteries.
The only reason
I'm still hanging around
Is to see what in hell
Is coming next.

TRIAL

I tried to be a boy.
I wore shorts.
I tied my braids
Behind my back.
I sat with my knees apart.
I tossed a ball while walking.
I kept my head down
When passing girls.
Was it because
I overheard my Father say
He had always wanted a boy?
I did try, Daddy.
I tried.

ELEMENTS

Gisela had an affinity
With the Chrysler Building
Almost from the inception
In the architect's mind.
She had an elongated figure
With blond, bobbed hair.
Her eyebrows shaded her
Deep set eyes from sun.
Corners in her flat were rounded
As she was, and
The brass and steel furnishings,
Shimmered
With their Egyptian motifs.
She bought everything in threes,
Her favorite number.
At night, she wore dresses of silver
With abundant gold jewelry.
She lived a fast and sleek life,
And became known for her
Neon lit parties and her
Martini glasses designed
With hand etched pyramids.
At her demise, a silver Bentley
Rolled down Lexington Avenue.
A gloved hand took
Gisela's ashes
From a golden urn,
Scattering them
Between 43rd and 42nd Streets.
One legend was gone.
The other still stands.

NO LISTING FOR NOWHERE

I ain't going nowhere.
No where's no good for me.
I gotta get to somewhere.
Some where's the place to be.
Say Mister, maybe you could help
By giving me a map,
Or pointing with your finger
And start me with a slap.
What's that you say?
A bridge ahead?
It's over a ravine
You're telling me?
Jump in, my boy,
I think that's pretty mean.
Heck, I know how to get somewhere.
You've changed me in a flash.
You'll see my name on billboards,
I'll be rich with lots of cash.
So long, goodbye you SOB,
I hope your life is grim.
You guessed
And got it right, old man.
I don't know how in hell to swim.

ACTIONS AND REACTIONS

If I moaned, he groaned.
If I pouted, he shouted.
If I interrupted, he erupted.
If I minced, he winced.
If I cringed, he unhinged.

Conversely,
If he fought, I bought.
If he smoked, I choked.
If he whitened, I brightened.
If he strayed, I delayed.

It was a never ending scene
Of a failed compatibility,
With a wearisome, daily interaction.
So farewell my dear Harry
And welcome Sebastian.
Shall we start, sweet Sebbie?
With you advancing
On me
While we're
Dancing?

A MOVIE BECOMES ME

If all the world's a stage
And humans merely players,
Am I then the audience
As I watch myself at play?

Tears will trickle as they do
But I have no taste of salt.
I watch my pain in others' eyes
But feel no jagged blade.
I hear laughter all around me
But I share no merriment.

I much prefer a movie screen
To view the daily cavalcade.
It matters not where I should sit
My popcorn's always next to me.

My world is black, I lie awake
To hear a tearful cry
It is my gentle heart, I know,
Asking for
FINIS.

O SHAKESPEARE

What did Shakespeare say
When he spoke
To we ordinary folk?
Did he speak as he wrote?
And was it all quotes
OR merely 'Have a good day.'

When he went to a pub
Did he feel he was snubbed
By his language so strange
And unfathomable.
Was he down to earth
Perhaps full of mirth,
When he said
'Guys, drinks are on me'.

Perhaps he paid two pence
For something worth one pence
Did he voice his 'O Villainy?'
Or did he smother his pride?
Be a good guy besides
And buy not just one, but buy three.

I wish I had lived near him
By chance to have met him
To Will, I'd be a sheer waste of time.
In all probability
Since I'm not nobility
I fear this is what he would say:
'Hit the road, wench, go astray, wench,
I have a play I must write today.'

ONE NEVER KNOWS

His name was Tony.

We met in an acting class

And given a scene

From a play to rehearse together.

During rehearsals

Tony became enamored of me

And I, not of him

One day, Tony said coldly

I have an Uncle

For me, he would do anything

To make you like me

Capeesh?

Frightened, I left the class

Two years later, I had married.

One day, my Mom phoned

Big news, honey, Tony called

I'll say, I said anxiously

What on earth did you tell him?

I said you were out.

Mom, I whined, I'm married now.

Well, dear, you never know.

IS ME ALL I THINK ABOUT?

At first
When you craved me,
It seems
That you crazed me.
Then
You delayed
Till you finally praised me.
Soon
You betrayed me.
That truly amazed me
And sadly, dismayed me.
Now you have strayed
And left my heart
Splayed.

I wish I had had enough saliva
To have spit in your face.

SWELLEGANT

I anguish over the almost
Disappearance
Of the word
Swell.
You look *swell* tonight.
Such an ebullient word
Would put a smile on the
Face of a somber recipient.
Where can *swell* be?
Buried in the pages
Of unread books?
Or floating in the galaxies
Waiting to hear
What a *swell* starry night?
Perhaps *swell* is in retirement
After being used for so long.
I am glad I was around
When both *swell* and I
Were popular.
I sure had a *swellegant* time.

RED TAKES A HOLIDAY

Maneuvering her walker
On the uneven, sloping sidewalks
Had been tiring.
She rested on her walker
Near a street corner..
To keep herself occupied,
She played a game in her mind.
When a red car appeared
She would end her repose
Black trucks, white limos,
Blue and purple cars.
Yellow taxis one by one
Beige and silver SUVs
But no red car.
Now a ghastly green
A veritable rainbow of colors
But No red car.
Hours passed.
Stubbornly, she waited,
For a red car.
It became dark.
Silently she rose
Homeward bound.
I'll play that game again
She thought
If I remember.

DOG DOINGS

I have to have a pooch right now.
A poopless pup, of course.
I have no time to walk him,
No leash is no remorse.

My dog will look like royalty.
He'll deign to wet his pants.
At five, he'll be behind the door.
My life will be enhanced.

He'll never need a hydrant
Or grass or any tree.
No need to rush from parties,
I'm calling him Godfrey.

At night, he'll be right on my bed
A living, breathing being.
He'll curl up, cozy, next to me
And bring on dreams of sex, oh gee.

I'm told there are no poopless pups.
So live alone, contented,
I'll wait, sit back, relax and pray
Until a no poop dog's invented.

NO REASON WHY

The earth lay in a brown
border around a field of
yellow wildflowers. Sun
turned the yellow into a golden
haze over the field. A breeze
caressed the flowers and rolled
across them like the waves on a sea.
A car parked alongside the earth's
border and a small child leaped
from the running board, and ran
squealing with delight, into the
yellow waves, her arms outstretched,
as if she were wading in water.
Those in the car watched as the
child almost disappeared. What
was missing was a painter with his
easel, capturing the beauty of the scene.
Suddenly, it became quiet, the sun
and the breeze had vanished, as had
the child. The echo of a gunshot was heard.
One could sense that nature was
outraged and deigned to bear witness
to what had occurred. Nothing
breathed.

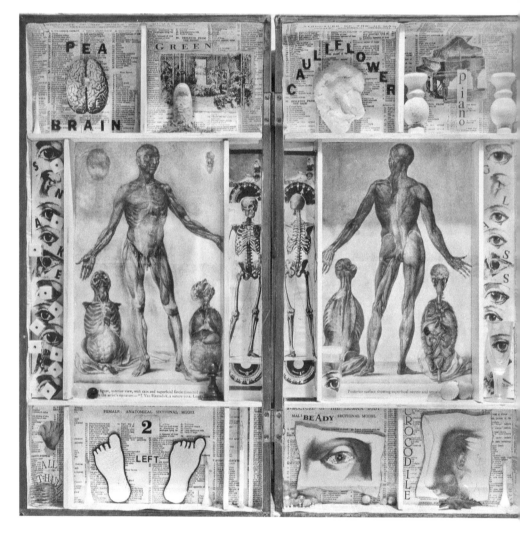

A COUPLE OF CLICHES

He had elephant ears,
Shed crocodile tears,
Had a face that would stop a clock.
Tick, tock.
Seemed never to mind
Until he met her,
She was different and very refined.

She played hard to get.
But in no time he knew
A few things, odd, about her.
It was hard to conceal
That she had nerves of steel
With snake eyes and a green thumb.
And on top of it all,
She had a trick knee
Which occasionally
Would make her squeal.

Plus he had a pea brain.
She played a shell game.
They married.
It seemed the right thing to do.
They started as lowbrows,
Soon became highbrows
And adopted only a pet.

A CHOSEN MOMENT

She took the love note
From its undisturbed nest
In a mahogany desk drawer.
The hand written note saw light
After decades of darkness.
Light made the yellowed paper
Cringe and begin to crumble.
As she read the written words
She sensed their passionate plea
To be remembered,
Before being swirled into their final ash.
She brushed the dust on the desk
Into the shape of a heart and thought
Was it only a moment that I loved him?
To hesitate is a moment
The blink of an eye is a moment
The sun dropping into the horizon
Takes only a moment.
In trying to recall her love, she hesitated,
Then blinked.
Through the window she saw the sun
Drop into the horizon.
Passion had blossomed and disappeared
Into her vast lifetime of memories.
Inwardly, she did remember loving him
Once,
For more than a moment
But now, love took only a moment
Or two.

UNSOLVED

Men remain a mystery to me.
Whoever let them come?
They're stubborn and do curse a lot
Yet some are handsome. Some.

Who'd ever want to wear their shoes?
There's enough that we must bear.
The sneaky ones wear sneakers
And run in underwear.

However do they pick their mates
And live with them for years?
Blondes and boobs are what they want
And legs; all three get cheers.

Underneath it all, I have loved men.
And found fun giving in.
So how to solve what makes them tick
Would be my mortal sin.

RITUAL

The midnight howl of a dog
Pierces the slim stem
Of his master's Martini glass,
Awakens the nearby neighbor
To his usual unpleasantness.
It streaks by
The virescent woodlands,
Challenging
The speed of light.
And failing,
The howl disintegrates
Drowning
In a shallow pool
Of nothingness.
The dog
Stretches and yawns,
Unaware
Of the sounds still
Tingling,
In the leaves above him.
Unaware that he has stolen
Silence.

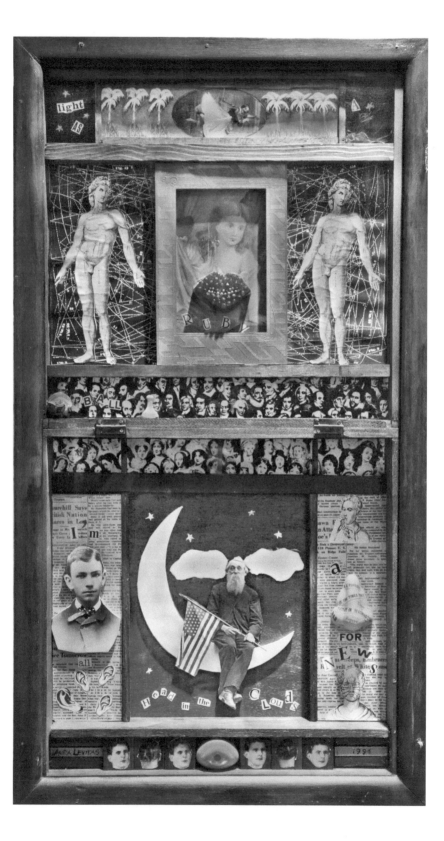

HIDDEN POCKETS

You entered the studio
wearing your trenchcoat,
a Brooks Brothersof course.
It was the in- coat of the decade.
It had a built-in disdain
which went with your disregard
for the morning greetings
from the staff.
The gaggle of actors outside
your office door,
grew quiet when you appeared.
If anyone spoke
they were asked to leave.
I was only a bystander
who watched the scene
and began to love your coat.
I wanted to wear your coat..
Your Brooks Brothers trenchcoat.
I wanted to have it dry cleaned.
Where is ut now?
Were you buried in it?
You should have been.
Or did it end up on the back
of a camel rider in Egypt?
Or Morocco?
Or on a hangar in a moldy, used
clothing store.
Your wife asked if I had loved you.
From my uncomfortable silence,
she knew.

THE STEPLADDER

Life is a stepladder
With indeterminate steps.
The first steps are growth,
Love and learning.
So since we do not know
When this learning
Process ends,
We continue to take each step,
With choices, courage
And commitment.
Then one day
We count the steps,
And to our amazement,
There are so many,
It is hard to fathom.
Yet we slowly recover
To step again,
Expecting not as many
Good times,
But happy to have
Climbed
So far

TIME STEP II

In my next life
I just want to be me.
I like being me.
It's been fun being me.
I don't want to come back
As an animal or an insect
Or a man.

I know I'll be back
But I don't want to
Start from scratch.
So who do I talk to
To explain what I want?
To guarantee what I get?
To make really sure
That I will actually,
Positively,
Be me.

ACKNOWLEDGEMENTS

Many thanks to STEVEN BOOKMAN, without whom this book would be without its cover.   His dedication and guidance in producing this book has made my lifelong dream come to fruition.

Thank you dear friend, INGRID EDWARDS, for supporting my first book and now continuing her praise and best wishes for my second.

DIRK SMILLIE, who is always there, with his help, interest and encouragement in getting my thoughts on paper.

My appreciation to ARTHUR MAKAR, my good friend, for his enthusiasm and assistance in all that I endeavor to accomplish.

Thanks to the photographers of my artwork included in this book: ADRIAN BUCKMASTER, PAUL DEMPSEY and JOSEPH AMELLA.

I am blessed with a supportive group of good friends, and my thanks go to all of them.

ABOUT THE AUTHOR

Aura Levitas is publishing her second book after an impressive debut in 2014 with her poetry and art book *Sisu* also published by the Vellamo Press.

Of Finnish background, Aura is the daughter of parents born on the same day and year near the end of the Nineteenth Century.

She trained as a dancer and appeared on Broadway in a number of musicals. The first of these was *Mexican Hayride* with lyrics and music by Cole Porter. She also attended the Chicago Art Institute, the Art Students League, and The New School.

As the Golden Age of television unfolded, Aura played a formative role in productions starring such legendary TV figures as Perry Como, Dave Garroway, and Milton Berle.

After her career as a dancer, she renewed her passion for mixed media and collage. Aura is a founding member of the Southampton Artists Organization, under whose auspices she has curated a number of shows. She has been exhibiting her art works both in New York City and in the Hamptons. She continues to create new work in her Greenwich Village studio.

PRAISE FOR *TIME STEP*

The work of a wonderfully gifted writer, Aura Levitas's poems in this new collection are a marvel and a delight -- charming, witty and wise.

> -- Thomas Meehan, Tony-award-winning Broadway librettist.

PRAISE FOR AURA LEVITAS'S FIRST BOOK *SISU* (2014)

I like these poems a lot. They are very spirited and poignant, revealing the inner life of an older person (showing that "old" is just a disguise for an ageless heart.)

> -   Annie Gottlieb

Aura Levitas has a natural rhythm in her words fitting together like shapes in her collages. An early experience with visual puzzles lends structural ambiguity to her lovely poems.

> -   L. Katz